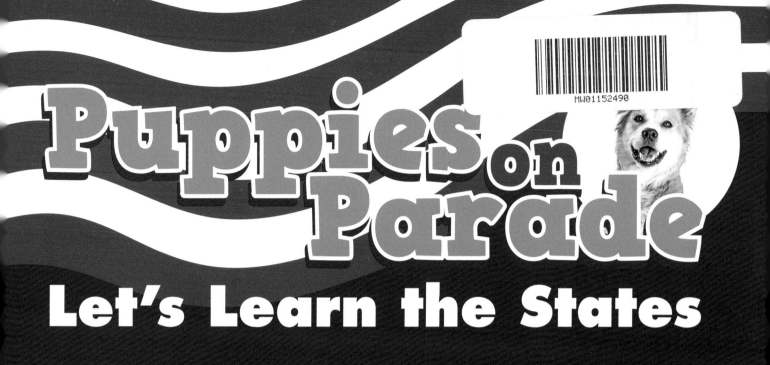

Puppies on Parade

Let's Learn the States

Julie Snodgrass and Meagan Martucci

This book belongs to

_____

For my wonderful grandchildren and all young learners everywhere.
—J.S.

For Jimmy and our amazing children. You're my world.
—M.M.

Requests for permission should be addressed to: Ascend Books, LLC, Attn: Rights and Permissions Department, 7221 West 79th Street, Suite 206, Overland Park, KS 66204

First Edition
10 9 8 7 6 5 4 3 2 1

ISBN: print book 978-1-73694311-3
Library of Congress Control Number: 2021937647

Cover and Book Design by Rob Peters

State Rankings by Size: Misachi, J. (2021, May 12). US States By Size. WorldAtlas.
State Rankings by Population: U. S. Census Bureau. (2021, April 26).
Historical Population Density Data (1910-2020). Census.gov

The goal of Ascend Books is to publish quality works. With that goal in mind, we are proud to offer this book to our readers. Please notify the publisher of any erroneous credits or omissions, and corrections will be made to subsequent editions/future printings.

Printed in The United States of America

www.ascendbooks.com

Puppies on Parade

Let's Learn the States

Hi there! I'm Darla the dog. Thank you for joining me on this adventure as we learn more about the great United States of America! I can't wait to introduce you to some of my friends as we journey together from state to state, learning interesting and useful facts along the way. Now let's get started!

AL

Alabama
Cotton State

Huntsville

Birmingham

Tuscaloosa

Auburn

Montgomery ★

Mobile

DOG HOUSE OF FACTS:

22nd State (1819)
30th in size
24th in population

**State Bird:
Yellowhammer**

**State Flower:
Camellia**

Carter the Collie says,
   "Welcome to my state!
The home of the Tide and War Eagle,
   I'm sure you'll think it's great."

Alaska
The Last Frontier

AK

Fairbanks

Anchorage

Juneau

State Bird:
Willow Ptarmigan

State Flower:
Alpine
Forget-Me-Not

DOG HOUSE OF FACTS:

49th State (1959)
1st in size
48th in population

The state of glaciers and polar bears is very nice.
Candy the Cavalier King Charles Spaniel loves playing in the snow and ice.

AZ

Arizona
Grand Canyon State

Flagstaff

Phoenix

Tucson

**State Bird:
Cactus Wren**

**State Flower:
Saguaro Cactus
Blossom**

**DOG HOUSE
OF FACTS:**

48th State (1912)
6th in size
14th in population

"Come visit the Grand Canyon,"
says the Dachshund named Dan,
"Cacti, tumbleweeds, and lizards
are all across my land."

6

Arkansas
Natural State

AR

- ● Fayetteville
- ● Fort Smith
- ★ Little Rock
- ● Hope

State Bird:
Mockingbird

State Flower:
Apple Blossom

DOG HOUSE OF FACTS:

25th State (1836)
29th in size
33rd in population

In his state is the only U.S. diamond mine,
Barney the Beagle thinks it's mighty fine.

CA

California
Golden State

CALIFORNIA REPUBLIC

**State Bird:
California
Valley Quail**

Sacramento

San Francisco

San Jose ● Fresno

Santa Barbara

● Los Angeles

● San Diego

**DOG HOUSE
OF FACTS:**

31st State (1850)
3rd in size
1st in population

**State Flower:
California Poppy**

"From the beautiful coastline
to some very tall trees,
the Golden State is the place to
visit," says Polly the Pekingese.

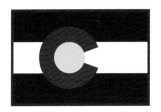

Colorado
Centennial State

CO

**State Bird:
Lark Bunting**

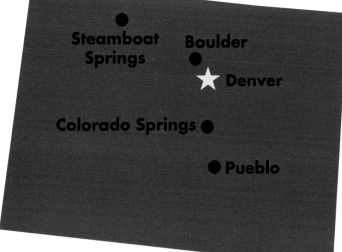

Steamboat Springs

Boulder

★ Denver

Colorado Springs

Pueblo

**State Flower:
White and
Lavender
Columbine**

**DOG HOUSE
OF FACTS:**
38th State (1876)
8th in size
21st in population

**Brenda the Brittany Spaniel loves playing in the snow.
The Rockies of Colorado are where she likes to go.**

CT

Connecticut
Nutmeg State

Storrs ●

★
Hartford

New Haven ●
Bridgeport ●

State Bird:
American Robin

State Flower:
Mountain Laurel

**DOG HOUSE
OF FACTS:**

5th State (1788)
48th in size
29th in population

The Maltese named Millie's state
is one of the original thirteen.
The uplands, lowlands, and beaches
are beautiful to be seen.

Delaware
First State

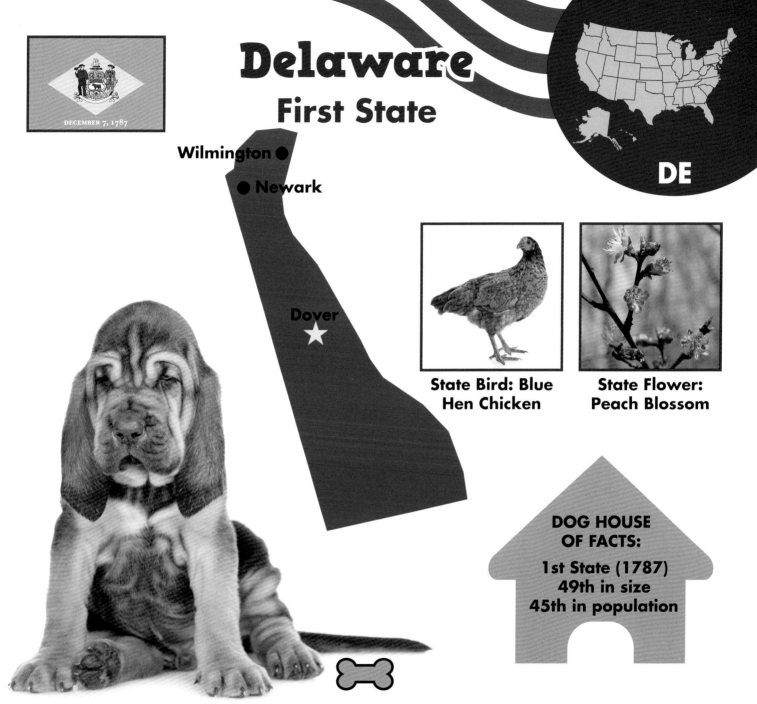

DECEMBER 7, 1787

DE

Wilmington ●
● Newark
Dover ★

State Bird: Blue Hen Chicken

State Flower: Peach Blossom

DOG HOUSE OF FACTS:

1st State (1787)
49th in size
45th in population

Bowzer the Bloodhound says, "I am from the First State. A day playing in the marshes is one I think is great."

Florida
Sunshine State

Jacksonville

★ Tallahassee

Orlando

Tampa

St. Petersburg

Palm Beach

Fort Lauderdale

Fort Myers

Miami

**State Bird:
Mockingbird**

**State Flower:
Orange Blossom**

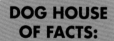

**DOG HOUSE
OF FACTS:**

**27th State (1845)
22nd in size
3rd in population**

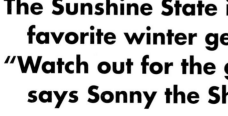

**The Sunshine State is a
favorite winter get-away.
"Watch out for the gators!"
says Sonny the Shar-Pei.**

Georgia
Peach State

GA

Atlanta ⭐

Athens ●

Augusta ●

● Columbus

Savannah ●

Albany ●

**State Bird:
Brown Thrasher**

**State Flower:
Cherokee Rose**

**DOG HOUSE
OF FACTS:**

**4th State (1788)
24th in size
8th in population**

**Penny the Pug's state has
peaches and peanuts,
Also the Masters tournament,
known for drives and putts.**

🐾 13

HI

Hawaii
Aloha State

Kauai

Niiahu

Oahu

Honolulu

Molokai

Lanai

Maui

Kahoolawe

Hawaii

State Bird: Nene

State Flower:
Yellow Hibiscus

**DOG HOUSE
OF FACTS:**

50th State (1959)
43rd in size
40th in population

The tropical beaches are
a favorite in this land.
Winnie the Whippet loves
running in the sand.

Idaho
Gem State

ID

**State Bird:
Mountain
Bluebird**

**State Flower:
Syringa**

● Lewiston

★ Boise

● Idaho Falls

● Pocatello

**DOG HOUSE
OF FACTS:**

**43rd State (1890)
14th in size
38th in population**

**Benny the Boxer loves the "Gem" of
the mountains; his state is tops.
There are lots of potatoes grown
here and many other crops.**

IL

Illinois
Prairie State

ILLINOIS

**State Bird:
Northern
Cardinal**

**State Flower:
Violet**

**DOG HOUSE
OF FACTS:**

21st State (1818)
25th in size
6th in population

Chicago ●

Peoria ●
Champaign ●
● Urbana
Springfield
★

● East St. Louis

**Illinois is the Land of Lincoln,
our 16th U.S. President,
Sammy the Schnauzer is
also a proud resident.**

Indiana
Hoosier State

IN

State Bird:
Northern
Cardinal

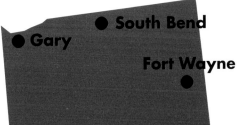

Gary

South Bend

Fort Wayne

Indianapolis

Terre Haute

Bloomington

State Flower:
Peony

DOG HOUSE OF FACTS:

19th State (1816)
38th in size
17th in population

"From the rivers of the south to
the northern dunes of sand,
my Hoosier home," says Cookie the Cocker
Spaniel, "is one of the best in the land."

17

Iowa
Hawkeye State

Sioux City
Waterloo
Cedar Rapids
Davenport
Des Moines

**State Bird:
Eastern Goldfinch**

**State Flower:
Wild Rose**

**DOG HOUSE
OF FACTS:**

29th State (1846)
26th in size
31st in population

"Welcome to Iowa," says the
Newfoundland named Nippy.
"In my state, the heartland farms spread
to the shores of the Mississippi."

Kansas
Sunflower State

KS

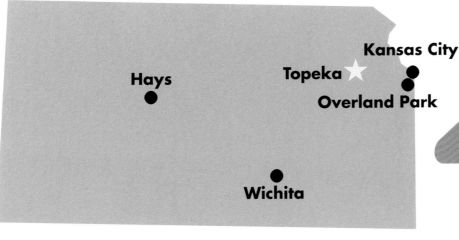

Kansas City
Topeka
Hays
Overland Park
Wichita

DOG HOUSE OF FACTS:
34th State (1861)
15th in size
35th in population

State Bird:
Western
Meadowlark

State Flower:
Wild Native
Sunflower

Sunflowers and prairies, the
state of Kansas has many.
"Come run with me in the Flint Hills,"
says the Lhasa Apso named Lenny.

KY

Kentucky
Bluegrass State

Frankfort ★

Louisville

Lexington

Paducah

DOG HOUSE OF FACTS:

15th State (1792)
37th in size
26th in population

State Bird:
Northern
Cardinal

State Flower:
Goldenrod

"The Bluegrass State is my home,"
says Jilly the Jack Russell.
"Mountains, horses and beautiful
spaces, I know it all so well."

Louisiana
Pelican State

LA

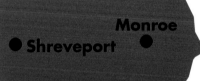

Monroe

● Shreveport

Baton Rouge ★

New Orleans

**State Bird:
Brown Pelican**

**State Flower:
Magnolia**

**DOG HOUSE
OF FACTS:**

**18th State (1812)
31st in size
25th in population**

"My state has many parishes, from
New Orleans to Shreveport,"
Vallie the Viszla says. "Swimming in
the bayous is a wonderful sport."

ME

Maine
Pine Tree State

State Bird:
Black-capped
Chickadee

Bangor ●

Augusta
★

Portland
●

DOG HOUSE
OF FACTS:

23rd State (1820)
39th in size
42nd in population

State Flower:
White Pine Cone
and Tassel

"Maine is my home," Guy the
Great Pyrenees boasts,
"from the forests to the rocky coast."

Maryland
Free State

MD

**State Bird:
Baltimore Oriole**

Baltimore ●

Silver Spring ●
Annapolis ⭐

**State Flower:
Black-Eyed Susan**

**DOG HOUSE
OF FACTS:**

7th State (1788)
42nd in size
18th in population

"We love playing in the water," say the
Komondors named Kel and Kay,
"from the Baltimore harbor to the Chesapeake Bay."

MA

Massachusetts
Bay State

Boston

Worcester ●

Plymouth ●

Springfield ●

State Bird:
Black-capped
Chickadee

DOG HOUSE
OF FACTS:

6th State (1788)
44th in size
15th in population

State Flower:
Mayflower

"The colonists were very brave,"
says the Papillon named Pearl.
"My home is full of U.S. history and
the 'shot heard round the world.' "

24

Michigan
Great Lake State

MI

Grand Rapids
Lansing
Detroit
Ann Arbor

DOG HOUSE OF FACTS:

26th State (1837)
11th in size
10th in population

State Bird:
American Robin

State Flower:
Apple Blossom

"Come explore my state,"
says the Mastiff named Midge.
"Visit both peninsulas as you
cross the Mackinac Bridge."

MN

Minnesota
Land of 10,000 Lakes

DOG HOUSE OF FACTS:

32nd State (1858)
12th in size
22nd in population

Duluth ●

St. Paul ●★
Minneapolis ●

Rochester ●

**State Bird:
Common Loon**

**State Flower:
Pink and White
Lady's Slipper**

"The lakes of Minnesota are
many to be found, and the
prairies and forests abound,"
says Bonnie the Basset Hound.

Mississippi
Magnolia State

MS

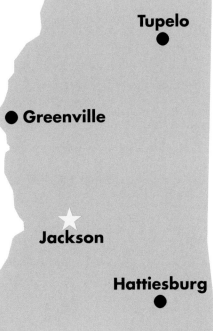

Tupelo

Greenville

Jackson

Hattiesburg

Biloxi

State Bird:
Mockingbird

State Flower:
Magnolia

"From the rich Delta lands
to the Gulf coastline,"
Ivan the Irish Setter says,
"I love this home of mine."

DOG HOUSE
OF FACTS:

20th State (1817)
32nd in size
34th in population

MO

Missouri
Show-Me State

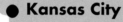

DOG HOUSE OF FACTS:

24th State (1821)
21st in size
19th in population

● Kansas City

St. Louis ●

★
Jefferson City

● Springfield

**State Bird:
Eastern Bluebird**

**State Flower:
White Hawthorn
Blossom**

28

**Ginger the German Shepherd says,
"From the City of Fountains
to the Gateway Arch, there
is so much to see.
Please don't forget to come visit me!"**

Montana
Treasure State

MT

State Bird:
Western
Meadowlark

State Flower:
Bitterroot

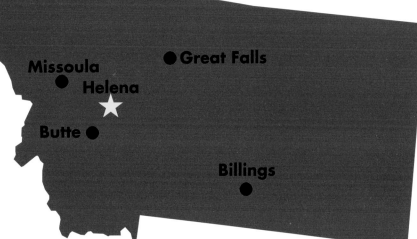

Missoula
Helena
● Great Falls
Butte
Billings

DOG HOUSE OF FACTS:
41st State (1889)
4th in size
44th in population

"The Treasure State has silver and gold."
Ruby the Rottweiler says, "At least
that's what I've been told!"

NE

Nebraska
Cornhusker State

State Bird:
Western
Meadowlark

Scottsbluff

Grand Island

Omaha

Lincoln

DOG HOUSE OF FACTS:

37th State (1867)
16th in size
37th in population

State Flower:
Goldenrod

Patches the Pointer's state is home
to the world's largest train yard.
Arbor Day and fields of corn
are held in high regard.

Nevada
Silver State

NV

Reno

★ Carson City

Las Vegas

State Bird:
Mountain
Bluebird

State Flower:
Sagebrush

DOG HOUSE OF FACTS:
36th State (1864)
7th in size
32nd in population

Duke the Dalmation wants you to know
that blue jeans were invented here.
You also may find gold and silver near!

NH

New Hampshire
Granite State

State Bird:
Purple Finch

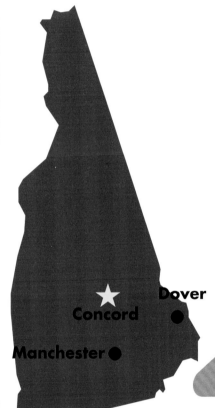

★ Concord

Dover ●

Manchester ●

State Flower:
Purple Lilac

DOG HOUSE OF FACTS:

9th State (1788)
46th in size
41st in population

Home of the nation's first wind farm,
Grover the Grey Hound thinks the granite formations
and quarries give his state a lot of charm.

New Jersey
Garden State

NJ

State Bird:
Eastern Goldfinch

State Flower:
Common
Meadow Violet

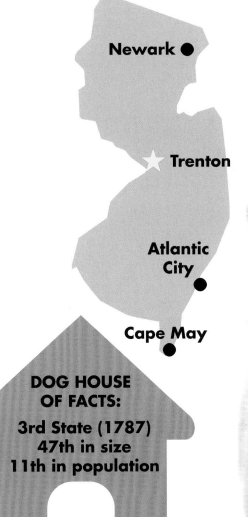

Newark ●

Trenton

Atlantic
City ●

Cape May ●

**DOG HOUSE
OF FACTS:**

3rd State (1787)
47th in size
11th in population

Home to beautiful beaches and the
longest boardwalk in the world,
Chuck the Chow Chow thinks his state is quite a pearl.

33

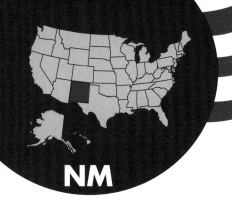

NM

New Mexico
Land of Enchantment

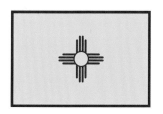

Santa Fe ⭐

Albuquerque ●

Roswell ●

Las Cruces ●

State Bird:
Roadrunner

State Flower:
Yucca

DOG HOUSE
OF FACTS:

47th State (1912)
5th in size
36th in population

The Rocky Mountains, forests, and
much wildlife running rampant,
Sassy the Saint Bernard loves
the Land of Enchantment.

34

New York
Empire State

NY

**State Bird:
Eastern Bluebird**

**State Flower:
Rose**

Syracuse

●Rochester   Albany ★

●Buffalo

●New York City

**DOG HOUSE
OF FACTS:**

11th State (1788)
27th in size
4th in population

In his state, Sheldon the Shih Tzu has much to do—
see the Statue of Liberty, tour the Empire State Building,
or catch a Broadway musical, to name just a few!

NC

North Carolina
Tar Heel State

NC

Greensboro

★ Raleigh

Asheville

Charlotte

Wilmington

State Flower:
Flowering
Dogwood

State Bird:
Northern
Cardinal

DOG HOUSE
OF FACTS:

12th State (1789)
28th in size
9th in population

Home to the Outer Banks and
flight of the brothers Wright,
Archie the Australian Shepherd likes to point
out, "Yes, we were the first in flight!"

North Dakota
Peace Garden State

ND

State Bird:
Western
Meadowlark

Bismarck ⭐   Fargo ●

State Flower:
Wild Prairie Rose

DOG HOUSE
OF FACTS:

39th State (1889)
19th in size
47th in population

Bandit the Bernese Mountain Dog's state is
known for its ranches and farms.
It's also the number one producer of honey,
so bees are no cause for alarm.

37

OH

Ohio
Buckeye State

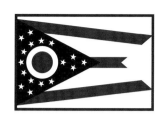

Toledo
Cleveland

**State Bird:
Northern
Cardinal**

Columbus

●Dayton

● Cincinnati

**State Flower:
Scarlet Carnation**

**DOG HOUSE
OF FACTS:**

17th State (1803)
34th in size
7th in population

When you visit Chloe the Corgi,
it really would be a shame
if you didn't make time to see
the Air Force Museum and
Rock and Roll Hall of Fame.

Oklahoma
Sooner State

OK

Tulsa●
Stillwater●
★
Oklahoma City

**State Bird:
Scissor-tailed
Flycatcher**

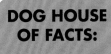

**DOG HOUSE
OF FACTS:**

46th State (1907)
20th in size
28th in population

**State Flower:
Mistletoe**

**Abby the Akita's state is known for
tornadoes and diverse terrain—
hills, lakes, forests, and the Great Plains.**

OR

Oregon
Beaver State

STATE OF OREGON

1859

Portland ●
★ Salem
Eugene ●

**State Bird:
Western
Meadowlark**

**State Flower:
Oregon Grape**

**DOG HOUSE
OF FACTS:**

33rd State (1859)
9th in size
27th in population

Known for its Wild West past,
Lola the Leonberger's state also has
scenic landscapes so vast.

Pennsylvania
Keystone State

PA

**State Bird:
Ruffed Grouse**

Allentown ●

Philadelphia ●

★ Harrisburg

● Pittsburgh

**State Flower:
Mountain Laurel**

**DOG HOUSE
OF FACTS:**

**2nd State (1787)
33rd in size
5th in population**

**Pepper the Poodle lives in the state
that is home to the Liberty Bell.
Pennsylvania is the chocolate
capital of the U.S. as well.**

41

RI

Rhode Island
Ocean State

Providence ★
Warwick●
Newport ●

State Bird:
Rhode Island Red
Chicken

**DOG HOUSE
OF FACTS:**

13th State (1790)
50th in size
43rd in population

State Flower:
Common
Blue Violet

**The Ocean State has scenic shores
and seaside colonial towns.
Sailing, surfing, and fishing—
Shep the Shiba Inu is totally down!**

42

South Carolina
Palmetto State

SC

Greenville

Columbia ★

Charleston ●

**State Bird:
Carolina Wren**

**State Flower:
Yellow Jessamine**

**DOG HOUSE
OF FACTS:**

8th State (1788)
40th in size
23th in population

Poppy the Pomeranian says,
"My state is home to arts
festivals and golf by the sea.
Also, there is nothing finer than a
tall glass of sweet iced tea."

SD

South Dakota
Mount Rushmore State

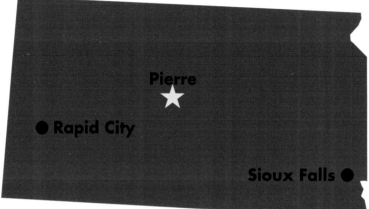

Pierre

● Rapid City

Sioux Falls ●

**State Bird:
Ring-necked
Pheasant**

**State Flower:
American Pasque**

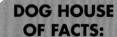

**DOG HOUSE
OF FACTS:**

**40th State (1889)
17th in size
46th in population**

"My home is known for tourism and agriculture," Harvey the Husky barks. "Mount Rushmore and the Badlands are among our national parks!"

44

Tennessee
Volunteer State

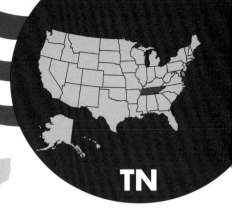

TN

State Bird:
Northern
Mockingbird

State Flower:
Iris

Knoxville

Nashville

Chattanooga

Memphis

DOG HOUSE OF FACTS:

16th State (1796)
36th in size
16th in population

The country music scene is strong in
Gary the Great Dane's home.
The Smoky Mountains and many lakes
provide great places to roam.

45

TX

Texas
Lone Star State

Lubbock

Dallas

Austin

Houston

San Antonio

Laredo

State Bird:
Mockingbird

State Flower:
Bluebonnet

DOG HOUSE OF FACTS:

28th State (1845)
2nd in size
2nd in population

The Lone Star State is big,
and the weather can be hot!
From the panhandle to the Alamo,
Benji the Bulldog likes it quite a lot!

46

Utah
Beehive State

UT

Ogden

★ Salt Lake City

Provo

State Bird:
California Seagull

State Flower:
Sego Lily

DOG HOUSE OF FACTS:

45th State (1896)
13th in size
30th in population

"From mountains to forests and deserts to canyons," Gabby the Golden Retriever says, "there is so much to see. We'll have so much to explore when you come to visit me!"

VT

Vermont
Green Mountain State

Stowe
●
★
Montpelier
● Burlington

State Bird:
Hermit Thrush

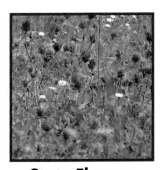

State Flower:
Red Clover

DOG HOUSE OF FACTS:

14th State (1791)
45th in size
49th in population

"My favorite type of syrup is maple,"
says Shawn the Sheltie.
"In my state, this is quite a staple."

Virginia
The Old Dominion

VA

Charlottesville

Richmond ★

Roanoke

Virginia Beach

State Bird:
Northern
Cardinal

State Flower:
Flowering
Dogwood

DOG HOUSE
OF FACTS:
10th State (1788)
35th in size
12th in population

Frank the French Bulldog
thinks his state is great.
The number of U.S. presidents born
here goes all the way up to eight.

49

WA

Washington
Evergreen State

State Flower:
Coast
Rhododendron

Seattle

Tacoma

Olympia

Spokane

DOG HOUSE OF FACTS:

42nd State (1889)
18th in size
13th in population

State Bird:
Goldfinch

Chico the Chihuahua says, "The name of my state is quite evident. I want you to know that it's named after the first U.S. president."

West Virginia
Mountain State

WV

**State Bird:
Northern
Cardinal**

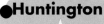

Morgantown

Huntington

★

Charleston

**State Flower:
Rhododendron**

**DOG HOUSE
OF FACTS:**

35th State (1863)
41st in size
39th in population

**Dexter the Dobermann
thinks running in the hills
and valleys are great.
This is why he chose to live
in the Mountain State.**

51

WI

Wisconsin
Badger State

WISCONSIN
1848

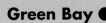

Green Bay ●

Madison
★
Milwaukee ●

State Flower:
Wood Violet

State Bird:
American Robin

**DOG HOUSE
OF FACTS:**

30th State (1848)
23rd in size
20th in population

"I hope you like cheese!"
says Bella the Border Collie.
She can tell you firsthand.
Her home is known as
America's Dairyland.

Wyoming
Equality State

WY

**State Bird:
Western
Meadowlark**

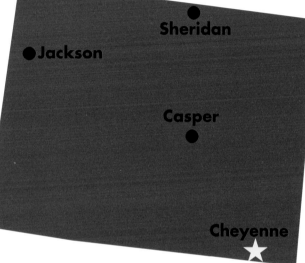

Sheridan

Jackson

Casper

Cheyenne

**State Flower:
Indian Paintbrush**

**DOG HOUSE
OF FACTS:**

**44th State (1890)
10th in size
50th in population**

Lucy the Labrador Retriever
sure does like to bark.
Her state is home to Yellowstone
and six other national parks!

53

Washington, D.C.
Our Nation's Capital

Bird: Wood Thrush

Flower: American Beauty Rose

DOG HOUSE OF FACTS:

Population 689,545
68.34 square miles

Allie the Airedale Terrier invites everyone to her home. Visit the monuments, museums, and the U.S. Capitol dome.

54

Oops! I was having such a dog-gone-good time showing you around this great country that I lost my stash of dog bones along the way!
Can you look back and find the bones buried throughout this book?
Once you find all 15 bones, please come back and tell me where they were hiding!
I've left space below for you to write which states you found my bones in.
I've also included some space for you to draw me a picture of a dog bone that I can add to my collection. Thanks, friend!

1. _____

2. _____

3. _____

4. _____

5. _____

6. _____

7. _____

8. _____

9. _____

10. _____

11. _____

12. _____

13. _____

14. _____

15. _____

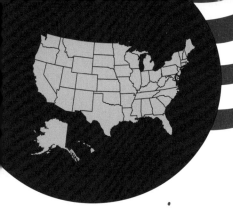

Pacific Territories

Pago Pago ⭐

American Samoa

Northern Marianas

Hagåtña ⭐

Guam

Saipan ⭐

Over in the Pacific where waters are often calm, There are 3 territories of the U.S. - Northern Marianas, American Samoa, and Guam

Caribbean Territories

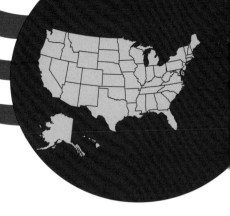

San Juan

Charlotte Amalie

U.S. Virgin Islands

Puerto Rico

And south of the continental 48 with
mountains and beaches of sand,
are the Caribbean territories of Puerto
Rico and the U.S. Virgin Islands.

Puppies on Parade

Take a look at all of our states! Do you remember the names of the states? Where do each of the puppies live?

Look at the map of the whole United States on the page before and fill in some of my water bowls below.

I put together a list of words to help me remember our time together, but it looks like they got all jumbled up! Can you help me unscramble them? That would be paw-some!

States where my family lives

States I have visited

I would like to visit...

States where I have lived

Word Scramble

1. upepspi _ _ _ _ _ _ _

2. dutnie tesast _ _ _ _ _ _ _ _ _ _ _

3. rlane _ _ _ _ _

4. ouejyrn _ _ _ _ _ _ _

5. forlew _ _ _ _ _ _

6. ruoynct _ _ _ _ _ _ _

7. apm _ _ _

8. idrb _ _ _ _

9. aglf _ _ _ _

10. atfsc _ _ _ _ _

11. guhdsoeo _ _ _ _ _ _ _ _

12. icsiet _ _ _ _ _ _

13. masniknce _ _ _ _ _ _ _ _ _

14. apsw _ _ _ _

15. silat _ _ _ _ _

```
Z A S N L A D W A C X V T E M P T U R A L K J O B F T A
F H R C D F S S D A J A L C R H V E Q I A M P R O V I Y
O L X K K D W M I L E U M A O D U A N N F Y V E I G W K
O V T C A U M A R I K R A W O I V E A N L O W G R G M C
A R I Z O N A S O F I N A T T U C I T C E N N O C M A U
M A I N E G S S L O F P N W N L S Q W W T S E N I Y R T
S N H Q Y O I A F R K D P U A I S Y T C Y G S C J B M N
Z I U X H A G C S N A R Q I U L O A O P A R H E R Y C E
F L S K H E V H F I M G O O S M E L R T M I V N E R B K
B O T X V V R U C A A P L Y I S O D O V G Q S T G Y H B
Z R E K G H Q S Z C B R V N W R I K J A T O S E N N I M
A A X O Y U U E N E A I G X A E A S N O C I X E M W E N
N C A D K B Q T U O L L P D N D N F S R X R M V V I C O
I H S R G L X T J W A L O O H L F H H I G U A P X S D T
L T N E B R A S K A K I C T F K Q H N N M O U Q D C N G
O U P O H I O H D X O N R Y M Q Q D E D V S R X U O O N
R O U J P X F O O T N O M R E V I W F N N S T G U N T I
A S A Z H U W D Z M N I K P E A J U E A E I U T E S G H
C Q M I M G N X N O A S T T N E D E C R W M A C U I N S
H W S L N Q I E A A E J E A R V A I Y J H H N T R N I A
T J O A Y I M D V L L J K S D K L X M H A J P S X L H W
R E W Z S G G A U A P S E I S J V J W N M T P B O N S F
O Y G N V N Z R R I D Y I A Y B F J A G P T Y V H L A I
N P K H A W A I I Y D A L E J F R T H G S T C B A W W B
N S Q U B R G K U V L A J A D W N C F A H V Y B V M C I
R S O U T H D A K O T A H E T O F Q U V I Z K E V W V W
A I N A V L Y S N N E P N O M W H I F O R P I C A V M T
W E S T V I R G I N I A Z D P L X R T A E D D P G Z O C
```

Can you find all 50 states and Washington, D.C. in this word search? Words can go in any direction. Words can share letters as they cross over each other. Have fun!

Alabama	Idaho	Minnesota	North Dakota
Alaska	Illinois	Mississippi	Ohio
Arizona	Indiana	Missouri	Oklahoma
Arkansas	Iowa	Montana	Oregon
California	Kansas	Nebraska	Pennsylvania
Colorado	Kentucky	Nevada	Rhode Island
Connecticut	Louisiana	New Hampshire	South Carolina
Delaware	Maine	New Jersey	South Dakota
Florida	Maryland	New Mexico	Tennessee
Georgia	Massachusetts	New York	Texas
Hawaii	Michigan	North Carolina	Utah

Vermont
Virginia
Washington
Washington DC
West Virginia
Wisconsin
Wyoming

Puppies on Parade

Fill in the blanks with the states and capital cities.

_ _ _ _ _ _ U _ _ _ _ _   **Boston is the capital of this state**

_ _ _ _ N _ _ _ _   **Barney the Beagle lives here**

_ _ _ _ I _ _ _   **This state is the Old Dominion State**

_ _ _ T _ _ _ _   **The capital of this state is Frankfort**

_ _ _ _ E _ _ _ _   **This is the home of Bonnie the Basset hound**

_ _ D_ _ _ _   **The Hoosier State**

_ _ _ _ S _ _ _ _   **Baton Rouge is the capital of this state**

_ _ _ _ _ _ _ T _ _ _ _   **A Maltese named Millie lives here**

_ _ A _ _   **This state is called the Gem State**

_ _ _ T _ _ _   **The capital of this state is Helena**

_ _ _ _ E _ _ _ _   **Gary the Great Dane lives here**

_ _ _ _ _ S _ _ _ _ _ _ _   **Harrisburg is the capital of this state**

Here's some more puzzle fun for you to share facts you've learned!

_ _ _ _ S _ _   The capital of Mississippi

_ T _ _ _ _ _   Penny the Pug lives in this state capital

_ _ _ _ A _ _ _   North Dakota's state capital is _____.

T _ _ _ _ _ _   The capital of the Garden State

_ _ _ E _ _   This is the capital of Alaska.

_ _ _ C _ _ _   The capital of New Hampshire

A _ _ _ _ _ _   The capital of the Pine Tree State

P_ _ _ _ _ _   Dan the Dachshund lives near this capital

_ _ _ _ _ I _   This is the capital of Washington

_ _ _ T _ _   The state capital of the Lone Star State

_ _ _ _ A _ _ _ _ _   This capital is where Sonny the Shar-Pei lives

_ _ L _ _   The capital of Oregon

_ _ _ _ _ _ _ _ S   This is the capital of Ohio.

ANSWER KEY

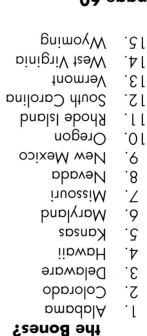

15. tails
14. paws
13. nicknames
12. cities
11. doghouse
10. facts
9. flag
8. bird
7. map
6. country
5. flower
4. journey
3. learn
2. United States
1. puppies

page 60
Unscramble puzzle

page 55
Where are the Bones?
1. Alabama
2. Colorado
3. Delaware
4. Hawaii
5. Kansas
6. Maryland
7. Missouri
8. Nevada
9. New Mexico
10. Oregon
11. Rhode Island
12. South Carolina
13. Vermont
14. West Virginia
15. Wyoming

page 62
States Capitals Quiz
1. MASSACHUSETTS
2. ARKANSAS
3. VIRGINIA
4. KENTUCKY
5. MINNESOTA
6. INDIANA
7. LOUISIANA
8. CONNECTICUT
9. IDAHO
10. MONTANA
11. TENNESSEE
12. PENNSYLVANIA

page 63
1. JACKSON
2. ATLANTA
3. BISMARCK
4. TRENTON
5. JUNEAU
6. CONCORD
7. AUGUSTA
8. PHOENIX
9. OLYMPIA
10. AUSTIN
11. TALLAHASSEE
12. SALEM
13. COLUMBUS

page 61

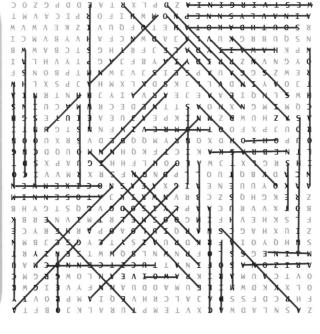

Thank you so much for joining me on this adventure. I hope you learned something new and exciting about the United States of America. My puppy friends and I enjoyed getting to show you around this great country we get to call home! Please come visit us again soon! Furwell, Darla